BBC M KU-736-926

Schubert Piano Sonatas

PHILIP RADCLIFFE

BRITISH BROADCASTING CORPORATION

Published by the British Broadcasting Corporation
35 Marylebone High Street, London W1M 4AA

ISBN: 0 563 07394 2

First published 1967
Reprinted 1974, 1977

Printed in England by Billing & Sons Limited
Guildford and London

I

1815–1819

The history of the piano sonata between 1750 and 1850 is of particular interest and contains some oddly contradictory features. Haydn and Mozart both wrote some magnificent specimens, especially in their later years; but, tantalizingly, during those years their sonatas become at the same time finer in quality and fewer in quantity, Haydn becoming increasingly preoccupied with the piano trio, and Mozart with the piano concerto. Even Beethoven, after completing his last five master-pieces, wrote no sonatas during the last seven years of his life. On the other hand there were composers such as Clementi and Dussek, whose work was inspired predominantly by the key-board, and whose sonatas, many of them of great interest and individuality, form the most important part of their output. Schubert comes somewhere between these two different ap-proaches. During his short life vocal and instrumental composi-tion played almost equally important parts; he found himself more slowly in instrumental than in vocal writing, but it was in his keyboard works that he was first able to do this, and the stream of piano sonatas flowed steadily until the three long and fascinatingly wayward works that he wrote during the last weeks of his life.

As a song-writer Schubert had the good fortune to be in a territory that had for over a century received very little attention from the greatest composers. In instrumental writing, on the other hand, he was concerned with forms that had already been used by the great Viennese classical masters. It was inevitable that his piano sonatas should be frequently subjected to com-parisons with those of Beethoven, and we have too often been presented with a rather depressing picture of the younger com-poser struggling desperately but unsuccessfully to free himself from the overpowering influence of his predecessor. Schubert had the deepest admiration for Beethoven and he could hardly be expected to have escaped the influence of his music, but it was equally impossible for so individual a composer to be oppressed or submerged by it. Towards the end of his life he wrote two movements whose structure follows that of two movements by

5

Beethoven with a closeness that must almost certainly have been deliberate. The Rondo in A major for piano duet is clearly modelled on the finale of Beethoven's Sonata in E minor, Op. 90, and the rondo of Schubert's Sonata in A (D.959)[1] on that of Beethoven's Sonata in G, Op. 31, no. 1; but in both cases Schubert's music is wholly characteristic and underivative. His independence from Beethoven resulted not from a tortuous and agonized struggle, but from his own innate individuality.

Colin Mason (*Monthly Musical Record*, September 1946) very rightly stresses the most important divergence between Beethoven and Schubert in their development of the piano sonata. Beethoven, having in his early years written sonatas on the same four-movement plan as his symphonies, did so less and less often in the later works, the only instance among the last five being Op. 106. Schubert, on the other hand, continued to use it on an increasingly large scale. This in itself was something of a challenge to the composer, as the piano, with all its great resources, cannot command quite the same variety of colour as an orchestra. In Beethoven's *Hammerklavier* Sonata the endless variety of texture gives to the music a kind of edge that precludes any suspicion of monotony. In Schubert's largest sonatas there is less of this; he seems, especially in the last four, almost to lose himself at times in a kind of rapt ecstasy. The writing is not always grateful to the performer and at the same time does not give much scope for the brilliant concert virtuoso. The sonatas can only make their full effect in the hands of a pianist who is able and willing to surrender himself wholly to the spirit of the music without any thought of display. They have many of the qualities that might be expected from a great song-writer: an immense fund of melodic invention and an equal inventiveness of attractive accompanying figures. Here, as in the songs, there is a very wide range of emotional atmosphere; one can find equivalents of the homely lyricism of *Die schöne Müllerin*, the deep melancholy of the *Winterreise* and the sinister dramatic power of such songs as 'Der Doppelgänger'. But here, as in all Schubert's larger works, these things do not always appear in the most likely places. The slow movement may contain music of a startlingly powerful and dramatic nature, the trio of the

[1] 'D' numbers refer to O. E. Deutsch, *Schubert: Thematic Catalogue of all his Works in Chronological Order* (London, 1951).

6

scherzo may be unexpectedly solemn, and the exposition of the first movement may include incidents and gestures of the kind that more normally appear in the development. Bearing in mind Schubert's temperament, it follows inevitably that a development section is always liable to contain lyrical passages, but this is by no means peculiar to him; there are familiar and wonderful instances in Beethoven, such as the first movement of his Violin Concerto.

Schubert's idiom, especially in his later works, is affected very much by his attitude to tonality. He hardly ever anticipates the kind of chromatic harmony that obscures the tonal outlines, but he takes great pleasure in travelling through remote keys, not as a means of producing dramatic tension, but just for the sake of the journey. He is liable during the course of a theme to go quietly and simply through modulations that an earlier composer would be far more likely to reserve for a moment of crisis; a familiar and remarkably beautiful instance is the second theme of the slow movement of the Unfinished Symphony. These passages often bring a sense of space similar to that produced by the sight of a distant view or by the sudden recollection of a far-off event, and they fit well with the leisureliness that becomes an increasingly prominent characteristic of Schubert's style in his later years. Equally personal is his attitude towards major and minor, whether tonic or relative; he is fond of hovering between the two, often with a strangely nostalgic effect.

His handling of sonata-form has frequently been compared, usually to his disadvantage, with that of Beethoven, one of the most familiar and misleading statements being that Schubert was unsuccessful because he preferred long flowing melodies to concise rhythmic figures. But Beethoven himself, in the first movements of his Violin Concerto, the first *Razumovsky* Quartet, the *Archduke* Trio, and others, was able to build the most majestic and satisfying structures on broadly flowing themes, and Schubert could on occasion use short rhythmic phrases as incisive as any of Beethoven's. But when this happens the rhythm does not permeate the movement as extensively as it would in a movement by Beethoven. For many people the word 'development' immediately suggests the fiercely and persistently argumentative procedure so familiar in many of Beethoven's extended movements. Schubert does not often adopt this; he is concerned more with presenting his themes against new harmonic backgrounds, sometimes turning them almost into different characters. Not infrequently an apparently new theme may grow imperceptibly out of another, with a subtlety that looks ahead to the methods of Brahms.

Examples of all these things will be found in the sonatas when they are examined in detail. But before doing this, it is worth considering for a moment their position in Schubert's total output. They are as characteristic of him as are the other branches of his instrumental music, and contain examples of every side of his personality, including the vein of naïvely cheerful conviviality that has sometimes been a stumbling-block to the more fastidious. Yet in the article already mentioned Mr Mason at the same time shows a generous appreciation of the musical qualities of the sonatas, and says, in the last sentence, that they have been forgotten 'outside the musicologist's study'. Even in 1946, when the article appeared, this was surely an exaggeration; there were already a fair number of pianists, including Schnabel and his pupils, who played the sonatas, and it is still less true now, when the Sonata in B flat has become almost hackneyed. But even so the sonatas have taken longer to win widespread appreciation than Schubert's other instrumental works. For many years they were criticized adversely for their length, but this should bring no difficulty to a generation that has accepted the symphonies of Bruckner and Mahler; and anyhow the best of the earlier sonatas could never be described as diffuse. On the whole, as has already been suggested, the basic objections are on pianistic rather than purely musical grounds. Many years ago a very famous virtuoso pianist, when advised to study Schubert's G major Sonata, promptly inquired whether it ended with an effective fortissimo climax and, when told that all the four movements ended quietly, lost interest. Deplorable though this may seem, the pianist's point of view cannot be ignored, and it is true that in these sonatas it is rare to find the kind of prolonged tonal build-up that makes the final page of Beethoven's Sonata in A flat, Op. 110, so thrilling for both performer and listener. The most notable instance is in the Sonata in A minor (D.845), and there it occurs at the end of the first movement, not the finale. In the sonatas Schubert is particularly fond of introducing a movement or a theme pianissimo; the direction *ppp* occurs frequently and *fff* only twice. With all their passages of dramatic power, the sonatas are basically intimate works, and this intimate note is harder for the player to sustain in large-scale works than in shorter and more concentrated pieces; sometimes he may experience the kind of frustration felt by a high-spirited dog that is straining vigorously at the leash.

It is interesting to turn for a moment to the Fantasia in C major (D.760), which at one time received far more attention from pianists than the sonatas. It is a powerful and original structure, containing some splendid music; there are in it passages that cater for the virtuoso more obviously than anything in the sonatas, and it is just at these places that the inspiration wears thin, especially in the rather clumsy final pages. Schubert was not a composer for the virtuoso, and it is significant that he is the only great composer of piano sonatas who never wrote a piano concerto. Had he done so he might have failed for the same reasons that caused his failure as a composer of opera. But this is no reason why the sonatas should not be enjoyed for their own merits.

The Sonatas of 1815–17

The earliest attempts date from 1815. By this time Schubert had composed a considerable amount of instrumental music. Three curious fantasias for piano duet ramble in a manner similar to the long dramatic ballads that he was writing about the same time. There are several string quartets, of very varying tendencies; sometimes rather incoherently ambitious, sometimes academic, with here and there a glimpse of the authentic Schubertian lyricism. The first two symphonies are more orthodox, but the Second is the best instrumental work that he had yet written. The first piano Sonata, in E major (D.157), which was written at the same time as the Second Symphony, was planned as a four-movement work, but the finale was either lost or not written. The first movement is not very distinguished in its ideas but has a characteristically spacious second group, which, as often in later works, falls into an ABA design of its own. But the other two movements are more individual, especially the vigorous minuet, the trio of which looks ahead to that of the much later Sonata in D major. The *andante* is in a gently elegiac mood not unlike that of Mozart's Rondo in A

9

minor. The returns of the main theme are attractively varied, the first being not an elaboration but a simplification, and the second making use of a figure from the previous episode.

The Sonata in C (D.279) is similarly incomplete, and, apart from some bold harmonic progressions in the first movement, is decidedly less interesting. But the five-movement work in E (D.459), which was written in August 1816, is far more attractive in every way. The gently lyrical first movement is more concise than those of its predecessors, and has many characteristic touches, such as the F double sharp on the last beat of the third bar, the alternations of major and minor near the end of the second group and the modulations in the development. About a year later its final bars somehow strayed into the song 'Elysium', possibly without the composer realizing what had happened. Perhaps owing to the presence of two scherzos, this work was originally published as *Fünf Klavierstücke*, but the subsequent discovery of the autograph makes it clear that Schubert intended it to be a sonata, though he may have felt uncertain which of the scherzos to choose. The first is on the whole the more striking, but it is of unusual character, being too large to need a trio, and it might be thought too weighty for its position. The *adagio*, which is the centrepiece, is the finest part of the work, and the exquisite modulation from E flat to A minor shortly after the return of the main theme must be quoted:

EX. 1

The finale, with the unusual direction *allegro patetico*, has some remarkable features, but compared with the rest seems slightly strained.

It would have been difficult, on the strength of these three works, to prophesy the future development of the piano sonata in Schubert's hands. The five-movement work in E major gives the most vivid foretaste of his mature personality, but it gives no indication of the remarkable variety that is to be found in the sonatas of 1817. They include some intriguing curiosities. One (D.557), not itself of much interest, begins in A flat and ends in E flat. Another, in E minor, has had a very strange fate. The first movement was published separately in 1888, the second (*allegretto*) in 1907, and the third (a scherzo) in 1928. In Deutsch's catalogue these three movements appear as D.566. Meanwhile, unexpected information came to light in connexion with the *Adagio and Rondo* in E major, published in 1847 as Op. 145. The *adagio* was found to be an abbreviated and mutilated version of an *Adagio* in D flat, and it transpired that an early copy of the rondo was headed 'Sonata Rondo'. It has therefore been assumed that the *adagio* in its original form was the lost slow movement of an incomplete Sonata in F minor written in 1818, and that the rondo was the finale of the Sonata in E minor. The work in this form has been edited and published by Kathleen Dale. The first movement and the scherzo are on the whole the best parts; the other two, though very pleasant, are rather repetitive, and their similarity of tempo and design tend to weaken the over-all effect of the work.

The most satisfactory of the sonatas of 1817 are undoubtedly D.537, in A minor, D.568, in E flat, and D.575, in B major, all of which are full of very attractive and individual music. In the previous sonatas personal touches can be found in a generally rather derivative idiom. In the best of the works of 1817 there are still signs of older influences, but the overall style has far more character.

Sonata in A minor, Op. posth. 164 (D.537)

The opening of the A minor Sonata is remarkable for its energy and for the very effective mixture of varied phrase-lengths. This is one of Schubert's most marked characteristics and is probably the result of his early preoccupation with song-writing. When an unimaginative composer sets metrical words, the rhythm of his music will be square and pedestrian; but for one of the calibre of Mozart or Schubert the setting of words will result in an increased subtlety of rhythm: in a typical operatic air by Mozart, such as Tamino's first song in *The Magic Flute*, the phraseology is more flexible and unexpected than is usual in his instrumental melodies. This asymmetry came to Schubert later in instrumental than in vocal music, but it became increasingly prominent, giving it an attractive waywardness. Equally characteristic, in the first movement of this sonata, is the exhilaratingly roundabout way in which Schubert moves from A minor to F major for the second group. This has a peculiarly nostalgic flavour resulting from the constant appearance of the flattened sixth of the scale; it is rounded off by a tune reminiscent of the opening of Mozart's String Quartet in D (K.575). This must have made a strong impression on Schubert, as it is recalled in the first two symphonies. It appears in the sonata with harmony so Schubertian that there is no suggestion of archaism. The development section is capricious in manner, and appears at first sight to have no connexion with the rest of movement. Harold Truscott, however, has pointed out (*Monthly Musical Record*, March–April, 1959) that it all grows from the last two notes of the exposition. As if to make amends for opening his recapitulation in an unorthodox key, Schubert ends the movement with a short coda in which the main theme makes a final and emphatic appearance in the tonic.

The first movement is the strongest part of the Sonata, and its moments of vivid dramatic suspense look ahead to the two later and greater works in the same key. The second movement is homely and lyrical, with a very characteristic main theme; this will be quoted later in connexion with the Sonata in A (D.959), where it reappears in a more spacious and subtle version (see p. 45). This movement is in a very simple rondo form, but with an unusual and very successful key-scheme: theme in E, first episode in C, return of theme in F, second episode in D minor, and final return of theme in E. The theme in its first return is, very characteristically, accompanied by semiquavers derived from the previous episode, and the final appearance comes very effectively after a gradual return from the remote key of D minor. The finale is also a rondo of a type common in Schubert's music, in which the second episode is a recapitulation of the first; it suffers from a tendency to garrulousness, but has some interesting points. The modulation from A minor to B flat near the opening recalls, in its procedure, Beethoven's *Appassionata* Sonata, but the atmosphere is totally different, Schubert being gently pathetic where Beethoven produces an atmosphere of awe-inspiring mystery. The coda makes admirable use of the repeated chords that announce the opening of the episode; they make a final dramatic appearance and then, turning into octaves, disappear into the distance before the sudden final crash.

Sonata in E flat, Op. posth. 122 (D.568)

The Sonata in E flat (D.568) is totally different; less bold, more relaxed, and showing Schubert in his most genially Viennese mood. Its composition, however, seems to have caused him some trouble. There is an earlier, incomplete version in D flat, with no minuet, and it was at one time thought that Schubert altered the key for fear that a signature of five flats might alarm the public. But the E flat version is not a mere transcription; there are significant alterations, especially in the developments of the two outer movements, and it is far more likely that Schubert considered the higher and brighter key more suited to the general character of the work. The first movement flows easily and amiably, with a comfortably convivial second subject. The piano writing is smoother and less varied than in D.537, with a liberal allowance of cantabile for the left hand. Here again the development has an improvisatory air, but it is possible to trace a connexion between the arpeggio figure on which it is mainly built and a similar figure in the exposition, and there is an ingenious telescoping of the main theme:

EX. 2

In the D flat version this movement ended with two loud chords which Schubert in the later version rejected as unsuited to the generally placid character of the work.

The gentle elegiac second movement seems happier in G

minor than in the more ponderous C sharp minor of the earlier version; it has an appealing pathos not unlike that of various movements by Mozart in that key, though the music is essentially Schubertian. The very melodious and graceful minuet has a trio that also appears in a scherzo in D flat which may at one stage have been intended for the first version of the Sonata. The finale returns to the genial mood of the first movement, though with a passing touch of melancholy in the second group. The development sections of the two versions of this movement are very unalike; the second is far the more attractive, but, as in the first movement of D.537, both are ingeniously derived from the close of the exposition. As a whole this Sonata has only occasional glimpses of the deeper Schubert, but it expresses his lighter and gayer moods with extraordinary charm, and is admirably unified in atmosphere.

Sonata in B major, Op. posth. 147 (D.575)

The Sonata in B major (D.575) is more varied and has an intriguingly unsettled air, as though Schubert was aware that his idiom was changing. This feeling of unrest may have been intensified by the very unusual choice of key. The first movement, in strong contrast to the smooth and symmetrical opening of the E flat Sonata, begins aggressively, with dotted-note rhythms and varying phrase-lengths. Soon the music takes a flying leap into the remote key of G major. A long second group follows, with a succession of melodies, during the course of which the tonality gradually moves from G to F sharp, and the dotted-note phrases give place by degrees to a gentler and more lyrical atmosphere. This is all carried out in an interesting and successful way, though without the extraordinary breadth and deliberation with which Schubert could do this kind of thing in later works. The development, built upon the opening phrases, begins in an arresting way with curious abrupt modulations, but it soon seems to lose momentum, and the unaltered recapitulation, starting in the key of the subdominant and ending without any coda, is something of an anticlimax. The movement as a whole, with all its attractive vitality, is slightly cramped, and a study of it may explain, to some extent, why Schubert's style in his latest works became more and more leisurely.

The *andante* has something of the same feeling of restlessness.

14

The opening theme, which surprisingly anticipates Mendelssohn's flavour, is followed by some very attractive modulations. The central episode opens with what appears to be a foretaste of the dramatic outbursts that occur in some of the later slow movements. Here, however, it only lasts for a few bars, after which the same thematic idea assumes an entirely different guise and forms the basis for a charmingly delicate dialogue for the two hands. In due course the earlier part of the movement returns, but after the excitements of the middle section a note-for-note repetition is impossible, and a background of staccato semiquavers continues almost unbroken till the end of the movement. The scherzo is of the same family as those of the two piano trios; it has the same contrapuntal liveliness and clarity of texture, though it has not quite the same dance-like character; the tiny trio has some very characteristic features, especially the unexpected F sharp major harmonies in the second half. The finale, in its early stages, has something of the same tonal restlessness as the first movement, but is far gayer and more relaxed, with an engagingly undignified second theme. But with all its light-heartedness it contains an admirable example of the way in which one thing can turn into another in Schubert's music. The three-note phrase with which it opens reappears towards the end of the second group with a new continuation, and at the beginning of the development the continuation detaches itself from the rest and turns itself into an apparently new tune. The process is shown in Ex. 3:

EX. 3

Allegro giusto

These sonatas mark the end of the first period of Schubert's development of the piano sonata. They are the most individual instrumental works that he had yet written, though they have not the grace and polish of the Fifth Symphony. On the whole the Sonata in E flat is the best of three, but the other two, though more unequal, are also more prophetic of later developments. All three deserve to be played more frequently.

Sonata in F minor (*D.625*)

By this time Schubert had become a very fluent writer for piano, and in addition to the completed sonatas of this period there are several that were left unfinished, and several separate movements that may have been intended for sonatas. The most interesting of these is the Sonata in F minor of 1818. The first movement, which breaks off at the end of the development, is built on a single theme treated most imaginatively; the modulations in the development are remarkably impressive. The main body of the recapitulation can be reconstructed quite easily, but it is harder to guess how the movement would have ended; the solution in Erwin Ratz's edition seems a little too easy. It is probable that the *adagio* in D flat, mentioned earlier in connexion with the E minor Sonata, was originally the slow movement of this F minor work. It is attractively rich in colour, and its key comes well between the F minor of the first movement and the very unexpected E major of the scherzo. Both this and the almost complete finale have strikingly original features, the opening of the latter giving a vivid foretaste of Chopin's Prelude in E flat minor. In the two outer movements of this work it is possible to feel a sense of conflict between the dramatic and lyrical impulses of the music – a conflict which was satisfactorily resolved a few years later in the first movements of two unfinished masterpieces, the String Quartet in C minor and the Symphony in B minor. But it is regrettable that this sonata was never completed, and very hard to believe that it was written only a few months later than the pleasant but much less adventurous Sixth Symphony.

Sonata in A major, Op. posth. 120 (*D.664*)

The next Sonata (D.664), in A major, was probably written in 1819, but the evidence is not conclusive. Though less ambitious, it is a subtler and on the whole maturer composition than the *Trout* Quintet, the only other large-scale instrumental work of that year. It is the most compact of all the sonatas, and one of the most endearing. The first movement opens in a lyrical manner not unlike that of the E major Sonata (D.459), and a glance at the two passages shows at once how much more individual Schubert's instrumental style had become during the last three years. Here there is nothing that suggests the work of an earlier composer, except for a reminiscence, in the second group, of the rhythm of the *allegretto* of Beethoven's Seventh Symphony, a movement that made a deep impression on Schubert. This second group begins, unusually, in the tonic, moving gradually into the dominant as it proceeds; this gives a peculiar feeling of continuity to the whole exposition. The movement is beautifully proportioned, with a development that is short but eventful. It introduces the one dramatic moment in the work, when the rising scale in triplets that originally preceded the second group appears in octaves in an unexpectedly aggressive guise. This outburst, however, soon subsides and gives place to a quietly conversational passage in which both the main themes take part. The opening of the recapitulation is introduced by a reference to the second strain of the main theme, which is in the relative minor; this gives a delightfully unconventional touch to the eventual return of the opening phrase:

EX. 4

In the coda, which consists of six bars only, the first theme makes a final appearance with gently nostalgic harmonies.

The *andante* is remarkable for its persistent use of a rhythm which frequently appears in Schubert's music, but normally in quick movements. Here it gives a sense of gentle persuasiveness which is enhanced by an attractive variety of phrase-lengths, sometimes of two and sometimes of three bars. It moves within a comparatively narrow range of key, but the modulation from F sharp minor to G major about halfway through the movement produces a magical change of colour, and there are some very characteristic alternations of major and minor. The finale is the most animated part of the work: like those of the Sonatas in E flat and B major, it uses full sonata-form, but with a very light touch. The themes are gay and lively, the second leading to some unexpectedly vigorous ramifications towards the end of the exposition. It therefore plays no part in the development, in which attention is divided between the first theme and an arpeggio figure that plays an important part in the transitional passage between the first and second group. The recapitulation opens in the key of the subdominant; here, however, this cannot be described as a labour-saving device, as it involves two striking modulations before the second is recapitulated in the tonic. Finally, as in D.537, the first subject makes a final return in the coda, which rounds off the movement delightfully. In some ways this sonata occupies a special position in Schubert's output. It does not aspire to the grandeur and dramatic power that are always liable to appear in the later sonatas; there are passages of gentle and appealing pathos in the first two movements, but the general atmosphere is lyrical and contented. Within its own limits, however, Schubert has here produced one of his most perfect works. The homely charm of the *Moments musicals* appears here on a larger scale, and the tuneful and flowing themes are fitted into sonata-form without any sense of strain. It is maturer and more personal in idiom than the earlier works, and its conciseness and concentration may commend it to those who are not in sympathy with the large and expansive proportions of the later ones.

II

1823–1826

Sonata in A minor, Op. posth. 143 (D.784)

Bearing in mind that it was as a song-writer that Schubert
approached composition, it is not surprising that his first wholly
individual piano sonata was predominantly lyrical in mood.
Between the A major Sonata and its successor, D.784, in A
minor, there is a long gap, during which his style in instrumental
composition increased greatly in scope. Mention has already
been made of the marvellous synthesis of the lyrical and dramatic
sides of his personality in the first movements of the Quartet
in C minor and the Symphony in B minor. The *Wanderer*
Fantasia of 1822 shows his remarkable skill at thematic trans-
formation, an aspect that has not always been sufficiently
realized. The latter months of 1822 were clouded by a serious
breakdown in health, and this may well be reflected in the
startlingly sombre tone of the A minor Sonata, written in
February 1823. The opening theme with its bleak octaves:

EX. 5

is far removed from the warm and genial colouring of the A
major Sonata. The atmosphere of sullen suspense is not unlike
that of Beethoven's *Appassionata*. Schubert's themes are apt to
fall into complete and independent designs of their own; the
first theme of D.664 is in a neat ternary shape, the central
strain being in the relative minor. In D.784 it is more elaborate;
the all-important phrase *x* from Ex. 5 turns into a persistent
accompanying figure, and introduces a march-like tune that moves
into the dominant. Then, after a crescendo, the opening theme
returns fortissimo, interspersed with scale passages in an
aggressive dotted-note rhythm which play an important part
in the development; the march-like tune then returns in the

19

subdominant, moving back to the tonic, completing a miniature binary structure. The rhythm of x dominates the starkly effective transition to the second group which is, rather unusually, in the dominant major. This is in a gentler mood, but before long there are reminiscences of x, with its second note elongated to a crotchet, and then of the first two bars of the main theme, punctuated by ominous silences.

The development is one of Schubert's tersest and most powerful. A magnificently broad expansion of the opening phrase leads to a furious outburst based on a combination of x and the dotted-note scales that appeared in the exposition. The tonality fluctuates in a very Schubertian way between F and D minor; the former key plays a very important part in the whole sonata. Once started, the dotted-note rhythm continues to dominate the development, but its mood becomes gradually less aggressive and it eventually forms the basis of a very attractive variation on the second subject. Finally it gives place to sombre reminiscences of the opening phrase which lead very impressively to the recapitulation. This has some unexpected features; the second subject is introduced more quietly, but it is given a more restless character by menacing triplets in crotchets. The coda is dominated by x; its appearance in augmentation produces an atmosphere of grim suspense that is resolved by a reminiscence of the vividly dramatic passage (omitted in the recapitulation) which originally introduced the second group. The movement ends quietly, in A major, but the final appearance of x, in double augmentation, produces a strangely hollow and enigmatic effect. Pianistically this movement is one of Schubert's hardest; so often the music calls for the more varied colours of the orchestra. But from every other angle it is one of the most powerful that he ever wrote and its construction is masterly.

The *andante*, like that of D.664, grows from a single theme, and it has none of the luxuriant spaciousness of Schubert's later slow movements. Its key, F major, comes very impressively after the end of the previous movement, and the broad melodic phrases of the theme are punctuated by a mysterious rhythmic figure in octaves. The second strain is worth quoting for the curious mixture of relative major and minor so characteristic of Schubert:

EX. 6

The rhythmic figure leads, with a grandiose modulation, to what appears to be a new theme, but after a brief climax it subsides into the humbler role of a counterpoint to the first theme, which reappears in the tenor register, moving as it proceeds from C to F. This is now less solemn in demeanour and the counterpoint lightens the colour: the rhythmic phrase appears over gently nostalgic harmonies that rob it of its oracular character. But it soon returns in its original octaves and the music hovers between various keys, looking back to the harmonies of Ex. 6. It is not until near the end that the first theme returns in its original mood, bringing the movement to a simple and impressive close. Few movements of Schubert say so much in so small a space; the atmosphere of solemn contemplation is reminiscent of some of the Mayrhofer songs, and it is particularly effective between the two stormy outer movements.

The finale builds an exciting drama round three very dissimilar characters. The first is a curling figure, not particularly individual in itself, but lending itself well to contrapuntal treatment; the second is vigorously rhythmic and liable to break out into rushing scale-passages; and the third is a gently lyrical tune with very characteristic touches both in harmony and in rhythm. The arrangement of these is skilful and original. The first two appear in A minor and the third in the F major to which this sonata so often gravitates. There is then a second presentation of all three, the first still in A minor, the second in E minor and the third in C major. A short development of the first theme follows, involving some very impressive modulations. Then the three themes make a third appearance, but in a different order; the first in A minor, the third in A major, and the second, in a

21

shortened form, in A minor. The work ends with a final dramatic stroke, the first theme appearing in unexpectedly aggressive guise in octaves; this is a passage of great technical difficulty, which should warn the player against setting a too precipitate pace. The key scheme is similar to that of the first movement of Beethoven's Quartet in A minor, Op. 132, and the general plan may have inspired that of the finale of Brahms's String Quartet in A minor. In few of Schubert's works does the more sombre side of his personality express itself with such concentrated power as in this sonata; it is an essentially tragic work that ends not in resignation or despair, but in a mood of fierce defiance. This tragic note can of course be found in other works by Schubert, earlier and later, but usually tempered more by gentler and serener elements. Here it has a peculiarly stark and biting quality that makes the sonata one of the most powerful of his works.

Sonata in C major (D.840)

The year 1824 was devoted mainly to chamber music: the Octet, the String Quartets in A minor and D minor, and the Sonata for piano and arpeggione. The only large keyboard work was the Grand Duo in C major for piano duet. But in 1825 Schubert wrote three piano sonatas, including the remarkable unfinished work in C major (D.840). In the first movement of this we meet for the first time in the sonatas the extraordinary spaciousness characteristic of his later instrumental music. It begins, like the Grand Duo and the A minor Sonata (D.784), with a very simple theme that is at first announced quietly in octaves and shortly returns loudly and emphatically. There is a touch of *Alice through the Looking-glass* in the masterly way in which the listener is led through a series of remote keys only to be landed no further afield than the chord of the dominant, and then, with a sudden last-minute twist, is spirited away to the unexpected key of B minor for the second group. The two main themes of the movement are not strongly contrasted; the second is accompanied by a rhythmic figure that has already been heard in the previous passage, and this gives a feeling of continuity to the exposition. This is further emphasized by the way in which the triplets of repeated notes that appear towards the end of the exposition are carried on well into the development. There is a characteris-

22

tic point in the development when the first theme (Ex. 7a) appears in a slightly altered form (Ex. 7b), with the last two notes going up, not down:

EX. 7

These two notes in their altered order are then detached from the rest and form the basis of a long argument. The recapitulation is introduced with great subtlety. The first theme is recalled without being actually restated, and it is only in its louder and more emphatic version that it appears in the tonic. The triplets that appeared at the end of the exposition do not reappear in the recapitulation, as there is no development for them to lead to; instead there is a long coda that refers to both the main themes. After a stately climax the movement ends, very unexpectedly, with a quiet recollection of the second phrase of the first theme. The whole structure is extraordinarily subtle and imaginative; all the points are made with the utmost breadth and deliberation, but the action never flags for a moment. The Olympian spaciousness of manner brings with it a suggestion of Beethoven, but the music itself is the purest Schubert, with his imagination at its most powerful.

The *andante*, in C minor, is hardly less remarkable, with touches of the sombre energy that is apt to appear in Schubert's later slow movements. It is in his favourite type of rondo form, in which the second episode is a recapitulation of the first; the main section is long-drawn and plaintive, with some very characteristic harmonic touches and modulations. The episodes are based on a quietly rocking tune that seems at first to have the character of a cradle song but is twice interrupted by fierce explosions. It returns to the more peaceful mood but continues, with a quietly menacing effect, as a counterpoint to the opening of the first theme when the latter returns. The repeat of the main section is varied, sometimes melodically and sometimes rhyth-

23

mically, in a way that emphasizes the restless undercurrent that characterizes the movement; the episode returns in C major, which gives it a brighter colouring than the darker and richer A flat in which it first appeared. The main section is much shortened in its final appearance, and there is a coda in which a curiously defiant effect is produced by B flats which seem, paradoxically, to emphasize the sombreness of the minor conclusion.

The incomplete minuet is a puzzling movement in which Schubert seems to have been hampered by diversity of material. It opens with a smoothly flowing tune, but this eventually gives place to the persistent rhythm that had already appeared in a slower tempo in the *andante* of the A major Sonata (D.664), and was later to play an important part in the minuet of the Sonata in G major and the first movement of the Piano Trio in E flat. It is possible that Schubert felt that these two very dissimilar elements made uneasy partners in a comparatively short movement, though this would have presented no difficulty in a large-scale sonata structure. On the other hand the short trio, in G sharp minor, has the inspired simplicity of the best of the *German Dances:* the single bar of B major in the first half is a beautifully characteristic touch, and equally effective is the wonderful distant glimpse of D major in the second half. The opening theme of the finale propounds a curious problem; it starts as a lively gallop in triplets which at the seventh bar is held up by duplets. Schubert must have felt this contrast of rhythms to be a stimulating challenge, but it is stressed with a persistence that becomes excessive. The elaborate treatment of the second theme also seems slightly forced, and the movement leaves one with the feeling that the ideas have somehow got out of hand. But there are delightful moments, such as the quiet passage at the end of the exposition, and the very Schubertian change from minor to major just as the movement breaks off. In his completion of the finale, Křenek makes it end quietly with a reminiscence of the first movement; thematic cross-references of this kind are not very common with Schubert, but the end of the Sonata in A major (D.959) supplies a possible parallel. The first two movements are undoubtedly the finest part of the work, and are indeed of magnificent quality. But in all four movements the writing is exceptionally orchestral in

24

character. There are, in Schubert's letters of this time, mysterious references to a 'grand symphony' on which he was working, and many people, from Schumann onwards, have supposed that the Grand Duo was a makeshift version of this; but the various orchestral versions of it that have been made have not been particularly successful, and in some ways it is more likely that the C major Sonata might have some connexion with the lost 'Gmunden-Gastein' symphony.

Sonata in A minor, Op. 42 (D.845)

The Sonata in A minor (D.845) contains nothing greater than the first two movements of the C major Sonata, but it is more consistently fine. The first movement in particular is one of Schubert's most powerful and original. It announces, in fairly quick succession, two themes: Ex. 8 which is wistful and melancholy, and Ex. 9, which is aggressive and military:

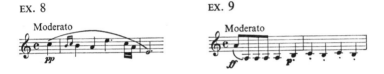

EX. 8   EX. 9

These are used in reverse order for the second group, Ex. 9 appearing in C major in a more urbane mood, and then Ex. 8 in C minor. With all his love for changes from minor to major, Schubert obviously felt that this theme would lose its character if put into the major. One of the most important problems for the pianist when playing it is to find a pace that is equally suited to both themes, without either rushing Ex. 8 or dragging Ex. 9. At the end of the exposition a new theme appears, deriving in its first three notes from Ex. 8, but it is quietly but firmly silenced by Ex. 9. At the opening of the development, however, this new theme is allowed a slightly longer say, though it soon has to give place, this time to Ex. 8, which dominates the development. First it appears in a gently lyrical mood, with a slightly smoother rhythm. Then, still in this altered rhythm, it is shifted to the bass and forms the basis of a dramatic crescendo followed by a sudden collapse. After a silence there is a gradual move towards the recapitulation, which is introduced as subtly as in the C major Sonata. Starting from the remote key of F sharp minor Ex. 8, in its original form, modulates through various others, one of which is the tonic, but at this stage there is no time for more than a passing glance at it. There is a reminiscence of the passage that led from Ex. 8 to Ex. 9 in the exposition, and finally Ex. 9 returns in its original aggressive mood in the tonic. The second part of the exposition is recapitulated almost exactly, Ex. 9 appearing in A major and Ex. 8 in A minor. The third theme then, as before, makes a tentative appearance, but after a pause the coda starts, and the third theme comes into its own. It begins to climb gradually from the lower register of the keyboard. The first attempt is soon suppressed by Ex. 9; the second, beginning an octave higher, leads to an angry outburst from Ex. 9 and a gentle protest from Ex. 8, making its final appearance. After the third attempt there is a more prolonged resistance from Ex. 9 until the final bars, when the third theme sweeps in grandly and has the last word. The whole passage achieves in a powerfully tragic mood what Schubert did on a larger scale and in a triumphant atmosphere at the end of the first movement of the C major Symphony; it is perhaps not surprising that the more tragic passage should also be the earlier in date.

The piano writing in Schubert's sonatas has sometimes been criticized for having too little polyphony, but that could certainly not be said of the second movement of this sonata. It is a set of variations, of which the theme itself, though simple and direct in manner, is subtle and sensitive in texture, especially in the way in which the tune is placed sometimes on the top and sometimes in an inner part. Towards the end the modulation to the supertonic minor and the nostalgic harmonies that follow it are particularly characteristic features. In the first variation the semiquaver movement makes the independence of the part-writing more apparent, and it leads to poignant harmonic effects. The first eight bars of the second half are here unaccountably reduced to four. The second variation opens with delicately decorative writing over simple repeated chords, but in the second half the texture becomes more contrapuntal; the touches of the minor at the cadences at the ends of both halves are very characteristic, and are perhaps intended to foreshadow the C minor tonality of the next variation. This is, emotionally, the climax of the movement; it is full of powerful clashes and suspensions which become more insistent as the variation proceeds. A particularly beautiful touch is the Neapolitan harmony in the third bar, which, when the phrase returns later, leads to a temporary glance at D flat, corresponding to the supertonic modulation in the theme. Here, as in several of Schubert's sets of variations, the minor variation is followed by one in the key of the flattened submediant (A flat). The fourth variation is the most brilliant, but there is some subtle and shapely line-drawing, and an undercurrent of explosive energy. It is followed by an exquisite passage in which the rapid demisemiquavers die away and the key returns to C major. The last variation has a wonderful serenity, with constant suggestions of distant horns. Towards the end there is a modulation to D flat that recalls the similar one in the minor variation. The coda, without any reference to the theme, contrives nevertheless to round off the whole set perfectly.

The scherzo is built on a theme which, as Maurice J. E. Brown has suggested, may well have been influenced by the fifth of Beethoven's *Diabelli Variations*. It is treated with a persistence which is saved from the slightest suspicion of monotony by constant rhythmic variety, phrases of five bars being used with particularly happy effects. Its high spirits make a welcome contrast to the thoughtfulness of the *andante* and the sombre energy of the two outer movements. The trio, much simpler rhythmically, has a gentle and dreamy tune that seems somewhere between a barcarolle and a *Ländler*. The finale has a strong affinity with that of Mozart's fine Sonata in A minor. It is in the same form, a sonata-rondo with a short central episode in the tonic major, and the same restlessness resulting from an almost unceasing quaver movement. Schubert's finale is particularly remarkable for its very spare texture; a considerable amount of it is in two parts, though often many more notes are implied. Here again there is great flexibility and variety of phrase-lengths; there is also great economy of material, the first episode consisting of phrases that have been heard before in a different context. Towards the end there is a striking anticipation of the famous second subject of the finale of the C major Symphony. The central episode, like that in the Mozart

27

movement, is in a concise binary shape of its own, but, as might be expected, Schubert's is the more leisurely. However, it is followed by a startling dramatic stroke when the apparently placid tune of the central episode appears fortissimo as a countersubject to the main theme. The third episode is a recapitulation of the first; after this there is no complete return of the first theme. This is unusual, but not surprising in view of the very full treatment, often with subtle differences, that it has had throughout the movement. In the coda it is recalled, with the phrase from the central episode sounded against it. The two final chords are almost identical with those that ended the first movement; there they came at the peak of a climax, and here as a sudden shock, but the effect is very satisfying and may well have been conscious. In any case this sonata has a strong feeling of overall unity, and from the player's point of view it is one of the most grateful. Temperamentally it is akin to D.784, also in A minor: less terse and enigmatic, more expansive and varied in mood, with touches – as in the final variation of the *andante* – of the strange visionary quality characteristic of the last four sonatas.

Sonata in D major, Op. 53 (D.850)

The last of the three works of 1825, D.850 in D major, is very different from the other two; it is brighter and more opulent in colour, perhaps more earth-bound, but a work of great vitality. Although dedicated to Karl Maria von Bocklet, a professional pianist, it is certainly not a conventional showpiece. It has a curious emotional scheme in which the heroically strenuous gradually gives place to the affectionately convivial. Naturally the former of these is the more prominent in the first movement, though there are glimpses of the latter in the second subject, which, however, does not play an important part in the general scheme. Thematically one of the less attractive of Schubert's first movements, structurally it is one of the most masterly. The main theme contains two important elements, one consisting of staccato repeated chords and the other of swirling quaver triplets prophetic of the Piano Trio in B flat. These present the same rhythmic contrast that somehow seemed to trip Schubert up in the unfinished finale of the C major Sonata. Here, where there is far less attempt at continuous melodic interest, the results are far more satisfactory. Although the musical inspiration is on a decidedly lower level, there is similarity, in the contrasted rhythmic elements and the unflagging energy, to the first movement of the C major Symphony; in both there are extraordinarily few silences, which is an unusual feature in Schubert's first movements. There is a wealth of modulation in the exposition, sometimes dramatic, as in the first few lines, and sometimes more lyrical, as in the delightful shift from A to B flat during the course of the second subject. But the most striking part of the movement is the development, which opens with a vigorous tune that grows from the repeated chord figure of the opening. This is soon worked contrapuntally with the quaver triplets, which continue almost uninterrupted, sometimes forming themselves into new melodic patterns, and sometimes providing a background to another new idea derived from the repeated-chord figure. The recapitulation is preceded by a period of prolonged suspense not unlike the equivalent passage in the first movement of Beethoven's *Waldstein* Sonata. After the recapitulation there is a short but very lively coda based on the vigorous tune with which the development began; the sudden chord of F sharp just before the end is a brilliantly characteristic touch.

The second movement, like that of the Grand Duo, looks back to the *larghetto* of Beethoven's Second Symphony; melodic reminiscences of it occur not only in the opening phrase:

EX. 10

but in many other places, and both movements are broadly planned and luxuriant in texture. But temperamentally they are less alike. Beethoven's movement, apart from a few moments of tension, is placid and contented, while in Schubert's there is a strong undercurrent of energy, which is not, as in so many of Schubert's slow movements, sombre and menacing, but fullblooded and happy. Although placed as a slow movement, it is headed by the unusual direction *con moto*, which suggests, not an unduly fast pace, but the necessity of maintaining to the full the rhythmic vitality of the music, without which the glowingly rich harmonic texture might cloy. Its form is similar to that of the *andante* of the C major Sonata – a rondo with the second episode recapitulating the first; the results, however, are very unalike. The earlier movement is tragic in character, with moments of lyrical relief provided by the haunting melody of the episodes; in the other, there is less contrast and the form is less clear-cut. At first sight it might give the impression of a delightful but rather inconsequent ramble from one idea to another; behind the wealth of luxuriant detail, however, there is much unobtrusive and ingenious planning, both the theme and the episodes being in a free ternary design. The key system is fascinatingly unconventional; during the course of the theme there are many incidental modulations, but the music always returns soon to the tonic. Just before its last cadence there is so strong a touch of subdominant harmony that the modulation to D major for the first episode has the air, not of a journey to an extraneous key, but of a return home. The episode contains two themes, both of which open with a melodic reminiscence of the *larghetto* from Beethoven's Second Symphony; for the second, Schubert goes yet another step further in the subdominant direction, to G major, and again somehow contrives to make this sound like a home-coming. When the episode has completed its design a delightful series of floating harmonies leads back to the theme, which is surrounded by ornamentation. The episode, in a shortened form, is then recapitulated in the tonic, and this time leads to a sonorous climax which stresses the vigorous syncopated rhythm that played an important part in the episodes. Having asserted itself so emphatically, it continues as a background to the final, abbreviated return of the theme; the last ten bars, in which the two of them die away, are of great beauty. For those who prefer the ascetic or the epigrammatic this movement may seem extravagantly rich, but its warmth and vitality cannot be denied.

It is in the scherzo that one can feel most clearly the gradual change from the strenuous to the more relaxed. The opening bars have a touch of the mock-heroic, and those that follow are in an amiably bantering vein. These two moods alternate, the latter being on the whole the more prominent and at one point taking shape in a delightful dance measure. In the trio, on the other hand, though there is no quotation, the music looks back to the opulent texture of the previous movement; the second half contains a magnificent chain of modulations which is full of the sense of vastness so characteristic of Schubert's maturest style. The repeat of the scherzo is followed by a coda based on the dance measure, and this is significant; for the rest of the work heroics are to be banned. The finale, with its engagingly frivolous opening, has sometimes been regarded as a kind of *enfant terrible*. Schumann remarked severely that anyone who took it seriously would lay himself open to being regarded as a laughing-stock. But Schumann, with all his devotion to Schubert's music, had his blind spots; he was misled by the gaiety and high spirits of the Piano Trio in B flat into thinking that it must have been an early work, and he was surprisingly cool even towards the last three sonatas. The finale of the D major Sonata, for all its light-hearted manner, is far from being superficial; it fills its basically simple design with a breadth and luxuriousness that make it an admirable foil to the equally broad and luxuriant second movement. In form it is a rondo of the older and simpler kind, with two episodes, the second of which is in a ternary shape of its own. There are a number of themes, very dissimilar in mood, but all beginning on the third beat of the bar; in fact the whole movement might be described as a development of the eighteenth-century *gavotte en rondeau*.

The theme first appears in its simplest form, the frequent dotted notes and triplets giving it an amiably jaunty air. The second strain grows in a very Schubertian way from the cadence of the first. In the first episode there is a masterly skill in the way in which the flowing semiquavers, appearing for the first time, become more and more insistent, gradually leading to a strenuous passage in invertible counterpoint, then returning to the earlier mood and finally trickling quietly into the return of the theme. This is now decorated with semiquavers deriving subtly, but not obtrusively, from the previous episode. This return is directed to be played 'con delicatezza', which is equally applicable to most of the movement. For the second episode the pace slackens and a new theme, beginning, like all the others, on the third beat, establishes a gently sentimental mood, which is emphasized by occasional 'Puccini octaves'. The rippling semiquaver background is reminiscent of some of the songs in

Die schöne Müllerin. This episode has its own central section, in which the theme that has just been heard is transformed into something far more aggressive, with abrupt modulations and indignant gestures. Soon, however, the tune resumes its amiable character and the main rondo theme returns for the last time. Now the decorating semiquavers are more persistent, and are accompanied, not by the original crotchet chords, but by quaver chords that give the whole passage a curiously fairy-like character. In the coda the semiquavers trickle away quietly, and the final bars recall, charmingly, the first phrase of the main theme in its original form.

Against the adverse judgements that have sometimes been passed on this movement may be set the opinion of Alfred Einstein, that it is 'the crown of the sonata'. It is perhaps easier for us now than it was a hundred years ago to realize that gaiety does not necessarily imply triviality, and that it is possible for a composer to carry out an emotional scheme of this kind without a feeling of anticlimax. Indeed, if we look at the Sonata as a whole, it is in the first movement, for all its powerful rhetoric and masterly construction, that Schubert gives us least of his most individual qualities. The second movement retains something of the grand manner, but tempered by a rich glow of lyricism. During the rest of the work Schubert moves with increasing happiness in the direction of friendly relaxation. With all .\s fine qualities, the Sonata in D does not show the extraordinary power and unity of the two great A minor works (D.784 and D.845); in some ways it looks ahead to the Sonata in A (D.959), which also has a massive and monumental first movement and a more relaxed and lyrical finale. There, however, the various elements are more integrated and the result more satisfying.

Sonata in G major, Op. 78 (D.894)

Of the many facets of Schubert's musical personality one of the most remarkable is a kind of mysterious serenity which can be felt deeply in such songs as 'Du bist die Ruh' of 1823, or the wonderful 'Im Abendrot' of 1824. In the piano sonatas of 1825 it appears occasionally, as in the theme and final variation of the *andante* of D.845, or in the very characteristic second theme of the episodes in the second movement of the D major.

But it finds more sustained expression in the next Sonata (D.894), in G major, which dates from 1826. Dedicated to Joseph Spaun, this is one of the most intimate of all his works, especially the first movement. In Schubert's later works the first movements usually go at a moderate pace; the *allegro vivace* of the D major Sonata is exceptional, and even in the C major Symphony the main part of the first movement is marked *allegro non troppo*. But in the G major Sonata the direction *molto moderato e cantabile* is unusually slow, and one of the most remarkable features of the movement is the way in which, despite its very leisurely pace, the action never drags. The magically beautiful opening has affinities with that of Beethoven's Fourth Piano Concerto in the same key, but the differences are soon apparent. Beethoven's theme has a stronger rhythmic element, and though in both movements the music floats quietly in and out of the key of B major soon after the opening, Schubert, as might be expected, does it with far greater deliberation, in a way that immediately commits him to the composition of a movement of considerable size. After the quiet solemnity of the opening it is inevitable that the second subject should be more animated; it is a broad, flowing melody with suggestions of a waltz rhythm in its accompaniment. It is at once repeated in a delicately varied form, and then followed by a descending scale passage leading to a chromatic harmony. Curiously enough Schubert had done exactly the same thing at the equivalent moment in the first movement of the E flat Sonata nine years before. There, however, the chromatic chord led to a modulation to a comparatively remote key; here its effect is simply one of colour. It is unusual in a Schubert first movement to find a second group that does not go through modulations of some kind; here, however, he remains firmly fixed in the dominant and ends with a fine codetta reminiscent of the opening of the movement.

The development introduces an element of tension that is necessary after so placid an exposition. The first theme appears in an unexpectedly aggressive mood, leading to a powerful climax; then the second subject appears, sounding in this context gentler than the first. The process is repeated, the first theme leading to a still more massive climax. The second subject reappears as before and itself assumes a more uncompromising guise in a contrapuntal passage in octaves. Eventually the quieter

C 33

mood returns and the development ends with a few bars that foreshadow beautifully the return of the first theme for the recapitulation, which, apart from the necessary key-changes, is very exact. The short coda is a wonderful example of what Schubert could do with simple tonic and dominant harmonies. In this respect, and in others as well, this movement looks ahead to the still more deeply contemplative first movement of the last sonata, in B flat.

The *andante* that follows is similar in form to those of the C major and D major Sonatas. Temperamentally it comes somewhere between the two, less sombre than the former and less luxuriant than the latter. The main theme is quiet and homely with simple but very telling harmonies. The episodes, which grow from a single rhythmic figure, show Schubert's skill in presenting the same character in totally different guises; there are some very characteristic hoverings between minor and major, and a peculiarly haunting refrain that recurs several times. But the very clear-cut binary form into which the two episodes shape themselves slightly weakens the effect of the movement as a whole, and gives an impression of repetitiveness that is not to be found in any of the other sonata slow-movements in this form. The theme on its first return is delicately varied; for its last appearance it is shortened, as in the slow movements of the C major and D major Sonatas. There are simple but curiously touching modulations to the subdominant and the supertonic minor, and finally a coda of eight bars that contains no direct reference to the main theme but has obviously grown from the rhythm of its first four notes, and makes a very satisfying conclusion. The movement contains much beautiful and powerful music, though it does not quite reach the exceptionally high level of its two neighbours. It can be seen from the manuscript of the sonata that Schubert originally planned a slow movement on a different theme, quoted by Maurice Brown in his biography of Schubert. It is in the same three-eight time as its successor, but is in B minor, the key eventually used for the minuet.

For this Schubert returned to the well-marked rhythm that had already appeared in the course of the corresponding movement of the C major Sonata; there it seems not to fit very happily into its context, and to be worked with a rather laboured persistence, while here its effect is irresistible. With all its rhythmic energy, it has a feeling of stateliness that differentiates it from the scherzos of the two previous sonatas. A fascinating feature is the little phrase of two bars that leads into the trio, anticipating its theme and thereby enhancing the effect of the modulation from B minor to B major. It is interesting to note that at the point where the rejected version of the slow movement breaks off there is a similar change from B minor to B major; Schubert may have felt that in this case it came too near the beginning of the movement to be effective. The trio of the minuet has an interesting musical descendant in the central section of Brahms's Rhapsody in B minor. There are resemblances of mood, melody and texture; in both passages the tune is given to an inner part, and the second half modulates quietly and beautifully to a remote key. Schubert sets himself a harder problem by doing it at a comparatively late stage, but then returns with a marvellous ease and simplicity. Of all the scherzos or minuets among the piano sonatas, this one comes nearest to the idiom of the short dances for piano, and it well deserves its popularity.

The finale has points in common with that of the D major Sonata; both movements are spaciously developed rondos with two episodes, the second of which is the more elaborate, and both end with quietly brilliant codas that in their final bars recall very happily the opening phrase. But the gaiety of the D major movement is of an essentially urban, Viennese kind, while in the G major the atmosphere is more rustic. It has not quite the variety or the engaging catchiness of the earlier movement, but it has a delightful feeling of open-air freshness, and beneath this there is a wealth of subtle and imaginative detail that is not always immediately apparent. An unusual feature of the main section is that it never leaves the key of the tonic and that its basic harmonies are all tonic, dominant or subdominant. Monotony is avoided by skilful variety of phrase lengths, and by occasional chromatic touches that derive from the first three notes of the theme. An important part is played by the little repeated chord figure that first appears in the third and fourth bar of the theme; it soon subsides into the background as an accompaniment figure, but reappears at the end of the section and has the last word before the music modulates to C major for the first episode. This is a kind of *moto perpetuo*, not

of the precipitate kind but consisting of an imperturbable
flow of quavers first in the melody and then in the bass. Here,
again, monotony is avoided by varied phrase-lengths and later
by odd, abrupt progressions that recur at the end of the section,
as in the curiously unfinal cadence:

EX. 11

which makes it clear that the music will not stay for long in C
major. The return of the main section has some interesting
modifications; at first the melody is in the tenor register, and
later there are some remote harmonic digressions which are
particularly effective in contrast to the very diatonic character
of the whole section in its first appearance. Again, the choice of a
near key for the first episode makes all the more telling the simple
but magical change to E flat for the second.

Here for the first time in the movement the music has settled
in a remote key, and it has the effect of an entirely fresh landscape.
The melody with which the episode begins is not unlike that of
the first episode, but has more grace and elegance. Soon it moves
to C minor to introduce a broad tune which is in strong contrast
to the rest of the movement. It is given twice over a flowing
accompaniment, the second time with decorations; then
fortissimo in the bass; perhaps the most Schubertian moment in
the whole sonata is when this tune appears quietly in C major
with deeply nostalgic effect:

EX. 12

Eventually, as in the equivalent section in the D major Sonata, the melody with which the episode began, reappears and returns very deliberately to G major for the final reappearance of the main section. This time there are no modifications until a very arresting modulation to B flat heralding the coda. This has a curiously ethereal atmosphere, with very delicate keyboard writing. Finally the opening phrase returns in a slightly slower tempo, and the repeated-chord figure has the last word.

The position of this work among Schubert's sonatas is not unlike that of Beethoven's Op. 95 among his quartets; chronologically it comes near the 1825 works, but, like the Beethoven F minor Quartet, it looks ahead to some of the characteristics of the latest compositions. Its generally intimate tone makes it an exacting work for the player, but also extraordinarily rewarding to one who is in sympathy with it.

III

The Sonata in G was originally published, without any authority from the composer, as a set of pieces, *Fantasia, Andante, Minuet and Allegretto*, and it has been thought by Schumann and some others, that the four *Impromptus* (D.935), were similarly intended by Schubert to be a Sonata in F minor. On the whole this is unlikely, especially as regards the first and fourth pieces. The fourth is brilliant and exciting, but far simpler in design than any of Schubert's later finales, and the first is not in sonata-form, but consists of a long and rambling exposition, followed by a slightly abbreviated recapitulation and a short coda in which the first theme makes its final appearance. To Schumann, however, this might not have seemed a fatal objection, as the first movement of his own Sonata in F minor, Op. 14, is very similar in plan to the Schubert *Impromptu* and may well have been influenced by it.

We are left now with the last three sonatas which, for many years, were regarded with a very qualified admiration. Schumann and Einstein were both cool in their approach, the latter para-doxically regarding the *Impromptus* of 1827 (or perhaps earlier) as Schubert's last word as a composer for tLe piano. Several English writers of the last century, such as H. F. Frost and J. S. Shedlock, wrote appreciatively of the sonatas of 1825–6, but considered the last three to be a decline. Even as late as 1927, a similar view was expressed in Hans Költzsch's *Franz Schubert in seinen Klaviersonaten* (Leipzig, 1927). They were written during an astonishingly short space of time, in September 1828, and the sketches for them that have survived show that composition for Schubert was not always the clairvoyant process that has been familiarized by tradition. Comparison of the sketches with the eventual versions shows that the changes were usually in the direction of expansion. In his later songs Schubert, generally speaking, aimed more at concentration; in his larger instrumental works, however, he was aspiring more and more towards an infinite spaciousness. For this music, as for Wagner's music-dramas, the listener must adapt himself to a slowly moving time-scale, and the works must be judged in terms, not of length or brevity, but of balance and proportion. Having been written in quick succession, the last three sonatas can be regarded as a group, and it is possible to trace a kind of emotional pattern running through it: the first, stormy and sombre, the second expressing a variety of moods ending with flowing lyricism, and the third serene and contemplative. There are certain traits common to all three: a remarkable breadth and simplicity of melody, an attraction to the key of C sharp minor, approached, of course, from very different angles, and a tendency to break into a rapid descending scale at moments of high tension. Between them they give a very complete picture of Schubert's musical personality in the last months of his life.

Sonata in C minor (D.958)

The Sonata in C minor (D.958) is the least known of the three; it is almost unrelievedly sombre in tone, but is a work of great power and individuality. The opening of the first movement immediately suggests the theme of Beethoven's Variations in C minor for piano, but the dissimilarities are more significant than the likenesses. Beethoven's theme, though full of energy is tersely symmetrical; Schubert's, beginning in a lower register, climbs further, eventually exploding in a downward-rushing scale. This feature, already mentioned, appears in some other late works of Schubert apart from these sonatas; it introduces the second subject in the first movement of the E flat Piano Trio, and provides a startlingly effective end to the last of the *Impromptus* (D.539). The fact that it occurs so soon in the first movement of the C minor Sonata is consistent with its generally stormy character. The first theme is repeated in a rather more lyrical form, but on the whole it plays a decidedly less important part in the movement than might be expected. The tempo indication is *allegro* but the fact that in the sketch it appears as *allegro moderato* is a warning against a too rapid pace, and it is essential that there should be no temptation to slow down the speed for the second subject:

EX. 13

39   (*continued*

EX. 13 (*cont.*)

This appears first in a mood of serene simplicity, but with characteristically subtle touches, such as the occasional introduction of a note over the melody, and the fleeting glimpse of D flat. It is repeated over a more restless background, and then forms the basis of an agitated passage which foreshadows the semiquavers that are so important a feature of the development. At this point chromatic touches become increasingly prominent, usually involving a rising semitone; they provide a curious tang to the final stages of the exposition, which consist of a haunting tune reminiscent of a phrase from the well-known song 'Ständchen' and finally of a reference to the last three notes of Ex. 13.

The development opens with a dramatic passage permeated by the same chromatic touches; soon the semiquavers break out, and an agitated series of modulations, with the rising semitone always in evidence, leads to what is perhaps the strangest feature of the movement – a mysterious chromatic theme:

EX. 14

Preceded by two bars of accompaniment, this is obviously intended to give the impression of a new character in the drama; its first three notes may have been connected in Schubert's mind with the melody of the second subject, but it is more probable that he felt it as the logical outcome of the previous chromaticisms. It continues for some time, in either the treble

40

or bass, accompanied by incessant semiquaver arpeggios. Eventually the arpeggios give place to chromatic scales in semiquavers, which add to the eeriness of the atmosphere. Then, when Ex. 14 has disappeared, the chromatic scales continue, and against them is heard in the distance the rhythm of the opening bars of the movement. A short crescendo culminates, very appropriately, in a downward-rushing scale, and the recapitulation begins. The earlier stages of this are compressed, the more lyrical version of the first theme being omitted. The second group, on the other hand, beginning in C major, is recapitulated in full; Schubert obviously felt a special affection for Ex. 13. After a very effective silence the coda reintroduces Ex. 14, in a more diatonic form, with the same background of semiquavers, and it is in this gloomily impressive mood that the movement ends. More remarkable than its occasional suggestions of Beethoven is its vivid foreshadowing of certain movements of Brahms, such as the first *allegro non troppo* of the Piano Quartet in C minor, which resembles it not only in the menacing atmosphere of its opening, but in the serene beauty and the generous treatment of its second subject.

For the second movement Schubert writes the direction *adagio* for the first time since the five-movement E major Sonata (D.459). It uses the same rondo-like form as the slow movements of the Sonatas in C, D, and G, but with more subtlety than the others. The main theme, in A flat, is solemn and leisurely; towards the end a chord of G flat minor introduces an element of mystery that is developed further in the later stages; it is followed by a curiously Verdian cadence which, until the end of the movement, always speaks in a whisper. The first episode begins with a melody of great spaciousness that moves from C sharp or D flat minor to E major. The passage in triplet chords that follows has a surface resemblance to a similar feature in the *andante* of the E flat Sonata; this misled Einstein into thinking that this movement should have been headed *andante*, not *adagio*. They continue for some time, through a chain of modulations, and, when the main theme has returned, they provide a background with some attractive chromatic touches. The mysterious G flat minor harmony is used this time as a kind of pivot-chord leading to the very remote key of A major, in which the theme ends. The second episode recapitulates the first in the expected way, but with great freedom. The melody begins in D minor and moves, like its equivalent in the first episode, to the relative major, but in a far more tortuous way. First it is accompanied by an agitated counterpoint in triplets; then in E flat minor, in the bass, with the counterpoint above it; and finally, in a towering passion, in F minor with the counterpoint below it in octaves. But after only three bars this mood subsides, in a strangely melting way, into F major. Everything is now a semitone higher than in the first episode, and the triplet chords show every sign of heading for A major for the return of the theme; this, however, is arrested at the last moment by a very impressive modulation. For its final return the theme appears in an inner part, with detached semiquavers in the bass, but it soon floats into remote harmonic regions, and once more the music seems on the point of settling in A major. It is rescued triumphantly by the Verdian cadence which for the only time in the movement is played forte; this is followed by a short coda of great beauty and simplicity. The total scheme, with its preoccupation with keys a semitone apart, is very characteristic of Schubert, and plays a particularly important part in the String Quintet in C major. The sketch of this *adagio* is complete, and a study of it shows how skilfully Schubert, in the eventual version, enhanced his original harmonic strokes by presenting them with greater leisureliness and deliberation.

The opening of the minuet seems so spontaneous that it is hard to believe that it was originally conceived without its flowing quaver accompaniment, in rather stolid block harmony. In a reticent and unassuming way this movement is as characteristic of Schubert as the rest of the work, especially in its subtly varied phrase-lengths. Particularly telling are the mysterious silent bars towards the end, one of which produces a curiously vivid sense of expectation between the minuet and the trio. This is a subdued and wistful *Ländler* in A flat, a key that has already been used for the slow movement, and will make a significant appearance near the end of the finale. In a work as generally dark-coloured as this sonata a lively scherzo could easily have been out of place: the minuet fits admirably into the general scheme.

The galloping finales of Beethoven's *Kreutzer* Sonata and Piano Sonata in E flat, Op. 31, no. 3, must have made a particular appeal to Schubert, and they have several descendants among his works, the earliest being the lively finale of the Third Symphony. The String Quartets in D minor and G major both end with movements of this kind; last, and far from least, comes the enormous finale of the C minor Sonata. Of these, only the movement from the Third Symphony can be described as wholly light-hearted; the two quartet movements combine high spirits with sinister and dramatic undercurrents, though the 'death' element in the finale of the D minor Quartet has sometimes been exaggerated. Abdy Williams in *The Rhythm of Modern Music*, written in 1909, described it as 'suggestive of the fun of the pantomime' which perhaps overstresses its other aspect. The finale of the C minor Sonata goes at a slower tempo (*allegro*) than any other of the movements; a too precipitate pace will lose the effect of many subtle harmonic details and will lessen the sense of inexorability which the persistent rhythm should convey. Though the opening theme suggests a rondo, the shape of the movement approximates more to sonata-form – on a vast scale and with great wealth of detail. Before long the music modulates through remote keys, including, significantly, D flat minor; then, quite unexpectedly, it returns for a moment to home-regions, the first theme appearing in C major. There follows a series of adventures that show in a fascinating way how themes can grow out of each other in Schubert's music.

There is a sudden and characteristic shift to D flat for a dramatic passage that culminates in a phrase of two detached notes. This proves to be the basis of the main theme of the second group, which starts in C sharp minor, and modulates with great deliberation through a series of keys, eventually arriving at E flat minor. Then a prominent cadential phrase quietly turns itself into an accompanying figure for a new melody in E flat major; this is one of the few moments of repose in the movement, and a passage of great charm. The last few notes of this are the germ from which grows a long and eventful development. First they turn into a new melody in B major, which forms itself into a self-contained binary form of its own. Then, after a leaping figure which recalls the rhythm of the first theme, the development continues in a far less lyrical way. The final phrase of the E flat melody is put through its paces in a series of sequential passages of subtly varied lengths, in a constant stream of modulation which eventually arrives at the dominant of C minor. The leaping figure returns and, after an impressive glance at the chord of D flat minor, the recapitulation begins. As in the first movement, the earlier stages of this are curtailed, the passage that came between the first theme and its recurrence in C major being omitted. The second group begins in B flat minor and works round to C minor, and then to C major for the restful tune that appeared before in E flat. But, just as the E flat tune led through an interrupted cadence to B major, so here, when recapitulated in C major, it leads to A flat, the key of the slow movement and the trio of the minuet. This marks the beginning of the coda, which, in a movement of this size, is inevitably planned on a broad scale. First there is a mysterious passage in A flat, built on the leaping figure, and based entirely on tonic and dominant harmony. Schubert had done something very similar at the equivalent place in the last *Impromptu* from D.935; in both cases the music, though quite undistinguished in itself, is extraordinarily impressive in its context, giving a feeling of vast spaciousness that contrasts vividly with its restless surroundings. As might be expected, the passage in the Sonata is the more leisurely of the two; it moves with great deliberation to the dominant of C minor, with (once again) a brief glance at D flat minor. Then, after a short pause, the first theme returns, and leads to the modulating passage which was omitted from the early stages of the recapitulation; after a brief climax there is a long diminuendo which is shattered at the last moment by two loud and sudden chords. For all its great length the proportions of the movement are remarkably well balanced; it is an astonishing achievement, combining an almost unbroken rhythmic impetus with a wonderful variety of content. Schubert's unfailing sense of tonal direction is shown not only in the surprising remote modulations, but also in the simple but singularly satisfying use of plain tonic, subdominant and dominant harmonies at the beginning of the second group.

Of the last three sonatas the C minor is the slowest to make its effect, and, except for the beautiful second subject of the first movement, it is perhaps the least arresting thematically. The brooding, sultry atmosphere of some of it is reminiscent of the A minor Sonata (D.784), but it is all on a far grander scale, with a more vivid sense of space. Of all Schubert's sonatas it is on the whole furthest from his familiar lyrical vein, but it expresses with remarkable power and breadth his darker and sterner qualities.

Sonata in A (D.959)

Although it contains nothing as extended as the finale of the C minor, the Sonata in A is longer as a whole; it is better proportioned, more varied in colour, and, of the last three sonatas, it gives the most comprehensive picture of Schubert's musical personality. The magnificent six-bar sentence with which the first movement opens sets an appropriately spacious atmosphere, but, like its equivalent in the C minor Sonata, it plays a comparatively small part in the general scheme. It is followed at once by Ex. 15:

EX. 15

which immediately brings a suggestion of mystery, and the whole exposition is planned with fascinating intricacy. Soon the last two notes of Ex. 15, made more incisive by the shortening of the crotchet to a quaver followed by a rest, detach themselves from their context and form the basis of an elaborate transitional passage. As in the first movement of the C minor Sonata, the rising semitone plays an important part. As the music approaches the second group, there is a shadowy phrase in the bass:

EX. 16

which is more significant than it at first appears to be. The second group opens with one of Schubert's simplest and most charming tunes, but he does not indulge it as he has done with the equivalent theme in the C minor first movement. Eventually the repeated notes in its second bar lead to a creeping fugato passage which rises to a climax with arpeggios reminiscent of Ex. 15. After a short silence the melody of the second group returns, ushered in by staccato quavers similar to those by which it was originally preceded; its third and fourth bars are repeated in a varied form. Finally the exposition is rounded off by a few quiet bars in which the theme of the fugato passage is combined with Ex. 16.

This elaborate scheme contains a certain amount that would be more likely to appear in a development section than in an exposition, and to decide upon the next step cannot have been an easy task. Schubert's solution is unconventional and entirely convincing. He takes the third and fourth bars of the second subject in the varied form in which they had just appeared, and presents them in an atmosphere so different from that of the exposition that they seem almost to be a new character. This development, like that of the first movement of the C minor Sonata, has a persistent background, which is by no means a common feature; here it consists not of semiquavers but of repeated chords. Against these the phrase from the second subject is expanded into sentences of varying length, but usually of five bars, with constantly shifting tonality. First it fluctuates between C and B; then it appears to settle in C minor, only to be wafted with a fascinating modulation to A minor. On the dominant of this key there is a long cresendo, with reminiscences of the first bar of the movement coming gradually nearer, and the recapitulation begins fortissimo. This, apart from some attractive harmonic digressions in the early stages, proceeds regularly until the coda. Here the majestic opening sentence appears in a higher register and a gentler mood, with some subtle references to its sixth bar; this is repeated an octave lower with a glance at F major. The effect of the whole passage in its context is extraordinarily moving. Just before the end a strange shadow is cast by a mysterious arpeggio on B flat, which seems to be the final reference to the rising semitone in the bass of Exs. 15 and 16. At last, with a prolonged arpeggio of A major, again reminiscent of Ex. 15, the movement ends quietly.

The *andantino*, in F sharp minor, is a remarkable instance of the dramatic power that is liable to be found in Schubert's later slow movements. It opens with a quiet barcarolle-like melody, simple but with unusual features, such as the moment when the first phrases reappear, unaltered melodically, but harmonized as though they were in A major. The whole passage is repeated with the melody an octave higher; this gives a sense of repose which makes the subsequent events all the more surprising. A recitative-like passage leads through shadowy chromatic harmonies to the very remote key of C minor. Various new phrases come and go, and the atmosphere becomes more and more sultry and menacing. After some abrupt key-changes the storm breaks with the rapid descending scale that was mentioned earlier as a feature common to all the last three sonatas. The music is now in C sharp minor, another characteristic of these works, and for a few moments it is almost incoherent in its wild intensity. Chromaticisms of various kinds occur but, though they add to the general feeling of turmoil, they do not affect the tonality. A dramatic silence is followed by a kind of recitative, which is at first interrupted by loud and violent ejaculations; eventually, however, the interruptions become less aggressive, and, with one of Schubert's most melting changes from minor to major, the music settles quietly in C sharp major. The stormiest part of the movement is now over, but it is clear that some time must elapse before the main theme can return. This is filled by a gentle and soothing passage, still in C sharp major, reminiscent of the *Impromptu* in G flat. The melody of this has a flowing accompaniment in semiquavers, which continues as a background to the main theme when it returns underneath some short rhythmic figures similar to those that accompany, rather more incisively, the return of the theme of the *andante* of the C major Symphony. But before long the semiquavers disappear, and, after a coda with some very expressive chromatic touches, the movement ends in profound gloom. An unusual feature is the way in which the rhythm of the third bar is varied; after the stormy central section the dotted rhythm of its third and fourth notes is ironed out into even semiquavers, and when it is referred to in the coda, the dotted rhythm is

47

transferred to the first two notes. Striking enough on its own account, this movement is particularly so in its context; it introduces a strange and almost terrifying element into a generally happy and triumphant work.

The opening of the scherzo, with its suggestions of pizzicato, is one of Schubert's most original ideas; it is followed by some surprisingly Chopinesque phrases. The atmosphere is gay and light-hearted, and it is therefore all the more startling when, in the second half, the music is wrenched violently from C major to C sharp minor, and a downward-rushing scale brings back for a moment the hectic atmosphere of the central section of the *andantino*. This is followed by a plaintive little tune based on the third bar of that movement, but a beautifully simple harmonic change leads back to the opening theme and mood, which becomes increasingly exuberant. The simple and charming trio foreshadows in its pianistic lay-out the opening of the *andante* of the Sonata in B flat, and in its melody there is a hint of the solemn central section of that movement.

The finale, one of Schubert's greatest, has several features of particular interest. It has already been mentioned that its plan follows very closely that of the rondo of Beethoven's Sonata in G, Op. 31, no. 1. In both movements the theme, after its first delivery, is repeated in the tenor register under a counterpoint of flowing triplets; the central episode is really a development section, and towards the end the theme appears in a broken version, followed by a coda in a quicker tempo. Equally interesting is the fact that for the main theme of this movement Schubert returned to that of the central movement of the Sonata in A minor (D.537). The two tunes are here quoted as Exs. 17 and 18:

EX. 17

Allegretto quasi andantino

It is fascinating to see how, in the A major Sonata, the simple phraseology of the tune in its earlier version is made more subtle and flexible by touches here and there. The sketch of this movement shows that for the first episode Schubert had originally used quite different material; it was built on short incisive phrases which were obviously meant to provide contrast to the flowing main theme. In its eventual form Schubert gets his contrast with music that is not less but more leisurely than what came before it. The melody of the episode is broad and flowing, not unlike that of the second subject of the first movement. It wanders happily through a number of keys and is surrounded by a constant flow of triplets; from time to time these form themselves into rising and falling arpeggios which, again, suggest similar things in Beethoven's G major Sonata. When the episode has run its course, the triplets continue; over them is heard the rhythm of the first three notes of the theme, and finally the first half of the theme returns grandly in octaves. The second half, however, only appears in the tenor version, under the triplet counterpoint. The second episode is far the most dynamic part of the movement, and is devoted entirely to strenuous developments of the first two bars of the main theme. After a series of modulations, the music reaches C sharp minor, the key to which Schubert is so often drawn in these last sonatas. Then there is a long-drawn ruminating passage which at one point seems to hover mysteriously between C sharp minor and E, but in due course settles very impressively in C sharp major. Soon the main theme returns, but this time there is no preparation, as it comes as a gentle surprise in F sharp. It quickly floats quietly back to its own key, where it continues unperturbed. The first episode is then recapitulated, and there is an eventful coda. There is a curious dream-like appearance of the theme, with silences between the phrases and glances at distant keys. Then the tempo quickens, and the last two bars of the theme are whirled through a variety of keys. After another silence, they are reiterated quietly over a tonic pedal and are then swept aside by a loud peroration which, without actually quoting, recalls vividly the opening bars of the first movement. This passage, coupled with the recollections of the slow movement in the scherzo, suggests that Schubert was here taking special pains to unify the whole work.

If this sonata does not quite reach the heights of the great work in B flat, it has more variety of mood and texture and, in the long run, there cannot be much to choose between them. It has already been suggested that there are points of contact between the Sonatas in A and D; both are big, opulent works in the grand manner, which tends to become less grand in their later stages. But in the D major Sonata the fine rhetoric of the first movement is rather impersonal, and, in spite of the beauty and warmth of the second movement, one can feel Schubert becoming more and more happily relaxed as the music becomes less heroic. In the A major Sonata on the other hand the grandeur of the first movement is tempered by other moods: the serene and simple beauty of the second subject and the curiously restless excitement of the development. And in the finale the flowing lyricism has behind it an underlying breadth and strength which makes the final bars seem not to be intrusively grandiose, but a summing up not only of the finale but of the whole work. The extraordinary outburst in the middle of the slow movement is unlike anything else in Schubert's music; even now, after so many subsequent developments, it still retains its strange, almost elemental power.

Sonata in B flat (D.960)

In the Sonata in B flat there is no place for terror of this kind. It looks back to the deep thoughtfulness of the G major Sonata, and the homely lyricism of the A major (D.664), and carries them to a sublime level. The opening theme resembles, in its serenity, the second subject of the first movement of the C minor Sonata, but with greater breadth and solemnity, which is enhanced by the mysterious distant trills. The tonal procedures are very characteristic. A quietly unceremonious shift from B flat to G flat leads only to a stately return to the tonic; then there is a much more emphatic leap to the very remote key of F sharp minor, and the second group begins. This moves gradually from F sharp minor to F major, much as Schubert had done eleven years before in the first movement of the B major Sonata. There the result, though lively and attractive, is slightly breathless; here it is accomplished with the utmost deliberation. At first it hovers between F sharp minor and A major in a manner particularly characteristic of the last sonatas; eventually it decides upon A major, and from there to F is an easy step. With so eminently broad and tuneful a first theme there is less need for sustained lyricism in the second group. Various ideas come and go, including an apparently frivolous theme consisting mainly of staccato arpeggios in triplets, which plays a surprising part later in the movement. Shortly before the end of the exposition the theme that first appeared in F sharp minor is recalled and turned into something far more solemn. In view of the length of the movement it is not surprising that the repeat of the first movement is seldom played, but the passage that leads back to it is remarkably powerful; here, for the only time in the movement, the mysterious trill that punctuates the phrases of the first theme appears fortissimo.

The development includes a greater variety of events than those of the other two sonatas. Again Schubert is drawn to C sharp minor, for a simple and very appealing melodic passage which is a kind of synthesis of the main theme and the opening phrase of the second group. Then the staccato arpeggios from the second group appear but with a far more purposeful air than before, resulting partly from touches of chromaticism, and partly from the presence of a new theme in the bass. After a series of modulations this new theme is turned into an independent personality of its own – a typically Schubertian example of one thing leading to another. An exciting crescendo, intensified by harmonic clashes, leads to Ex. 19, which is still based on the new theme, and hovers attractively between D minor and F:

EX. 19

The fluctuating tonality produces a strange sense of distance, which is still more noticeable when, against the continuing repeated chords, are heard first the trill and then the first four bars of the main theme. The tonality is still a rather restless D minor, but very slowly and deliberately it glides into the dominant of B flat; eventually the development ends on a suitable note of expectation with the trill sounding quietly in the bass. The recapitulation contains some modifications; the digression to G flat that came early in the exposition now goes further afield, but still returns to the tonic. The coda, recalling the main theme, is of the utmost serenity and beauty, the trill making a wonderfully timed final appearance, just before the end. This one of the longest and quietest of Schubert's first movements, but its gentle manner and leisurely procedure conceal the highest mastery of composition.

Schubert's later slow movements often show a remarkable dramatic power, those of the String Quintet in C and the Sonata in A (D.959) being perhaps the most striking instances. That of the Sonata in B flat is one of the profoundest that Schubert ever wrote, but it is also one of the most subdued; its general mood suggests 'the still, sad music of humanity'. The main theme has a melodic similarity to those of the slow movements of the Piano Trio in B flat and the String Quintet:

but the three are presented against such dissimilar harmonic backgrounds that they appear as totally different personalities. In both the Sonata and the Quintet the tune is surrounded by accompanying figures above and below, and in the Sonata this has an almost hypnotic effect. Once more it is in C sharp minor, but here again, as in the *andantino* of the A major Sonata, the melody soon reappears, unaltered melodically, but harmonized as though it were in E major. And a little later a phrase that first appeared in E major is harmonized in C sharp minor. This attractive ambiguity emphasizes the gently resigned atmosphere of the music. In the sketch of this movement the melody of the central section appears in the tenor register, with animated figures over it; in the final version it is still in the lower half of the keyboard, but supported simply by rich and solemn harmony. There is at one point, just before the return of the main melody of this section, a passing reference to the cadence that ended the first section; in its context this has a curiously dream-like effect. Eventually the main section returns, but with striking differences. The accompanying figure is slightly more animated, and at the moment when the music had previously gone into E major it now goes, with thrilling effect, to C major for a short time. Not long afterwards there is a simple but deeply moving change to C sharp major, and the movement ends in deep serenity. It would be hard to imagine a more perfect sequel to the first movement; in both of them Schubert is at his most profound, with a brooding, visionary quality astonishing in the work of so young a composer.

A scherzo of the more boisterously energetic type would have been out of place in such a context. On the other hand, in view of the moderate pace of the first movement, something more brisk than a minuet is required. Schubert solves the problem by writing a scherzo of fairy-like delicacy, full of delightful melodic phrases that appear sometimes in the treble and sometimes in the bass. In the second half there are very characteristic modulations going through D flat and A; the return from the latter key to B flat is accomplished by a chromatic step than can hardly be called a modulation at all. The main part of the scherzo ends almost in mid-air and the change to the much more sombre atmosphere of the trio, in B flat minor, is electrifying. The lively quaver movement ceases, and there is a curious sense of foreboding due largely to the cross-rhythms and the ominous-sounding detached notes in the bass. The unceremonious way in which the music goes into D flat at the end of the first half, and the cadence at the end of the second, are very characteristic of Schubert's latest style; the latter has a decided foretaste of Brahms. For the first time since the D major Sonata, the repeat of the scherzo after the trio is followed by a coda. Here it is much shorter, consisting only of three quiet chords of B flat, which, however, contrive somehow to round off the movement perfectly. It is very unlike any other of Schubert's scherzos. Its impish delicacy may owe something to the scherzo of Beethoven's *Hammerklavier* Sonata, Op. 106, but in that movement there is a decided undercurrent of ferocity, of which there is no trace in Schubert's scherzo.

The finale, like those of the *Trout* Quintet and the Grand Duo, opens with a held octave and, as in the Grand Duo, the tune that follows pretends at first to be in the wrong key. In the sonata Schubert, following in the footsteps of Beethoven in the finale of his String Quartet in B flat, Op. 130, begins as though in C minor. The octave G with which the movement opens is far from being a mere call to attention; it has the air of being a kind of static commentator on the actions of the other characters, who towards the end proves to be less static than has been imagined. The movement on the whole is in a lighter vein than the finales of the other two sonatas, but it is full of vitality and is more imaginative than might be thought on first acquaintance. The playful opening contains some characteristic touches, such as the delightful digression to A flat, and the perfectly timed intrusions of the octave G. It is in the same form as the finale of the A major Sonata, the first episode being of great length.

First there is a sustained tune that might almost be a chorale, were it not accompanied by a lively semiquaver figure, with detached notes on unaccented beats in the left hand. When this has formed itself into a complete design of its own, there is an unexpected outburst in the minor, with a downward-rushing scale. The tune that follows, however, proves to be blustering rather than really formidable, as it soon relaxes into an amiably jocular mood in the major, over a triplet accompaniment; in this guise it could almost be a frivolous relation of the finale of the C minor Sonata. After an abbreviated return of the theme there is a central episode which, as in the A major finale, is devoted to development of the opening phrase; there is some vigorous contrapuntal writing and, near the end, a curious dallying in the key of the tonic, which is only made possible by the tonal ambiguity of the theme. After the first episode has been recapitulated, there is a comparatively short coda in which, for the first time, the octave G moves first to G flat and then to F. The final stages are brisk and incisive, the rhythm of the main theme asserting itself to the last.

If this work does not cover quite the same range as the A major Sonata, its emotional scheme is beautifully balanced, the gaiety of the finale being a perfect counterpart to the rapt contemplation of the first two movements. It does not aim at the dynamic power of the C major Symphony and, of the other late instrumental works, the one with which it has most in common is the String Quintet in C. Both works have the same ecstatic quality; in the Quintet it bursts more frequently into flame, while in the Sonata it is gentler and more reserved. To suggest that the last three sonatas were conceived as a consciously planned tripytch would be far-fetched, and a performance of all three of them in succession would put an impossible strain on both pianist and audience. But it is fascinating to trace the gradual increase of serenity from each work to the next. When, in the finale of the Sonata in B flat, the familiar descending scale rushes down the keyboard, it suggests nothing more than a passing outburst of temper that soon evaporates, while the gentler mood that first appears in the second subject of the first movement of the C minor Sonata becomes stronger and more sustained, and eventually finds it glorification in the Sonata in B flat. Though all three works contain magnificent music, the last reaches the highest level and rounds off wonderfully Schubert's career as a composer of instrumental music.

Since Schubert's death many composers have written piano sonatas, but few have produced more than a small number. Later in the nineteenth century there have been some undisputed masterpieces, such as Chopin's in B flat minor and B minor, and Liszt's in B minor. And those of Schumann and Brahms contain much fine and characteristic music. The most prolific composers of sonatas since then have been Russians, Skryabin, Medtner and Prokofiev: very different personalities, but all in their own ways writing sonatas intended mainly for the concert virtuoso. In Schubert's sonatas this element counts for very little; they owe their existence not to any concern with public performance but simply to his irresistible urge to compose. It is their essential intimacy, sometimes combined with an almost limitless sense of space, that gives them their peculiar fascination, and for those in sympathy with the music, this fascination is perennial.